This book is dedicated to my best friend Brad, who made my 3 years at university unforgettable.

Illustrations and images produced by Rosella Hazeldine.

I would also like to thank my specialist mental health mentor Catherine Gregory, De Montfort University and my counsellor Neil Hargreaves, De Montfort University, who have both helped with my own internal processing and a clarity of my experiences.

Contents

THE WAY OUR GARDENS GREW, SO DIFFERENT.

Intoxicated

/ɪnˈtɒksɪkeɪtɪd/

adjective

Drunk or under the influence of drugs.

Intoxicated to me is a very strong word. Sometimes it is something we do to alleviate pain or forget about something that has happened or that is ongoing. Some of us can act irresponsibly when *intoxicated*, losing control of our behaviour and disregarding how this affects others. From a young age, I was exposed to someone who would be *intoxicated* regularly and as a result, I felt the impact of having the safety of both myself and that person compromised. It's something I'd never expect my children to have to face.

Intoxicated

Intoxicated
by Satan's nectar.
Chronic but normal,
we only suffer.

Till the cold morning air-
reality strikes.
You don't show me real love,
that's something I'll never know.

The way our gardens grew,
so different.

Intoxicated

Intoxicated.
Your presence, so
precious.
I never forget you.

When there's bad days
I won't tell you.
I won't show you.
Because I'm your mother.

The way our gardens grew,
so different.

Him

/hɪm/

Pronoun

Used as the object of a verb or preposition to refer to a male person or animal previously mentioned or easily identified.

The pronoun *him* means to me someone who is strong, supportive and reliable. This is something I missed out a lot on during preteen years when my parents broke up and moved apart. I was lucky to eventually move out of my mother's home to live with my dad and have that father figure again. Once you have one, a father figure is hard to replace. This is made impossible when men other than your Dad come into your life and pose a threat to your safety and happiness. As a mother, providing for your children should always be of priority, so letting a new partner into the home should only happen when it won't put already tenuous circumstances at further risk.

Him

The fuel
to complete disarray.
Bangs and shouts
destroy happiness.

You let her habits continue
even when I was scared.
But, with your bulged pockets
you didn't care.

The way our gardens grew,
so different.

Him

Your love,
exudes into our home
so ubiquitous –
it warms our hearts.

Incessant good deeds
remind me of you,
the man,
I joined in holy matrimony.

The way our gardens grew,
so different.

Memories

/ˈmɛm(ə)ɹiz/

Plural noun

Something remembered from the past.

The *memories* you hold close should not be the ones where you can only tell half of the story for fear of it sounding tainted to those who hear them. They're something that should be recalled for the joyous times they've brought in their entirety. They're something you should look forward to creating with the people you love and share those invaluable moments with.

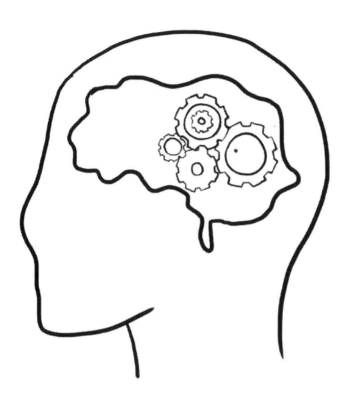

Memories

Memories
even in that dark place,
we had fun.
All we had was each other,
my best friend, my brother.

But we don't talk about it,
it stays alive within,
I still feel it
when it beats in the darkness.

The way our gardens grew,
so different.

Memories

When I rest
they do not come,
when they do,
not a sigh.

I always know
tomorrow the same.

They're hard to pull out
when the roots are strong.
The way our gardens grew,
so different.

Hope

/həʊp/

Noun

A feeling of expectation and desire for a
particular thing to happen.

Hope to me is the everlasting light. However, you
can't always count on its worth, for sometimes it
can be false. Those times may be ones where we
don't make the effort for something positive to
happen and other times may be due to too much
wishful thinking. When you get older, I think your
relationship with h*ope* becomes more pragmatic.
You can become too attached to *hope* when you are
younger and this exposes you to being let down
time and time again. I guess the cycle continues.

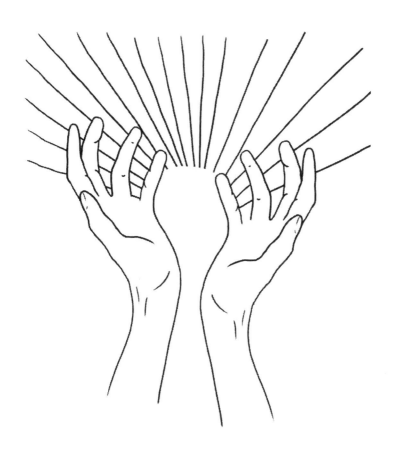

Hope

Your little faces
the hand paintings,
the cries.
Now I can't hear you
in these walls.
You were my hope,
the stars that shone
so stark.

I still count on you
to keep the
fire alight,
when there's nothing.
I pray for a better tomorrow.
The way our gardens grew,
so different.

Hope

This season will be different,
my eleven.

The march
down White Hart Lane,
I'm in that crowd.
Whatever the score, I'll be proud.

If I'm there,
Audere-est-facere!

The way our gardens grew,
So different.

Survival

/səˈvaɪv(ə)l/

Noun

The state or fact of continuing to live or exist, typically in spite of an accident, ordeal, or difficult circumstances.

Survival to me is a challenging concept to face. It is unfair that at times in my life, particularly preteen years I was faced with moments it felt like I was surviving rather than living and as a result it has contributed to how I respond to things today. Sometimes, this has been through the flight freeze response, where you feel paralysed and are incapable of controlling your feelings appropriately. However, you can always pull the weeds out and commit to dealing with things differently and more healthily. I find that refreshing.

Survival

Safety is priority.

I daren't speak
but my heart -
that does it for me.

Don't cry.
I give everything my all
and there I am, the child,
searching...

That hope the meal
won't be so bare.

Now I yearn for the comfort,
I needed in abundance.
The way our gardens grew,
so different.

Survival

Exposed,
to dissolving certainty,
the encounter
breathes in vicinity.

Our rhythm,
the bodies in motion
distracted in tracks of mire,
a shady character in the distance.

We take shelter
amongst the nylon tissues
they keep us nested
for our stay is short.

The way our gardens grew,
so different.

Tears

/tɪə/

Noun

A drop of the salty liquid that moistens the eyes and inner eyelids and that flows from the eyes when someone is crying.

Tears are usually an indication to the self of what is important to us and poses the question: Are we focusing on the right thing? It is even more humiliating as a male to shed *tears*, although it shouldn't be. Nevertheless, there will always come times where people will see your weakness. Try not to forget those *tears* that once fell have only made you stronger and have built the person you see in the mirror every day.

Tears

Even in my escape,
I couldn't hide them,
they were the
stain on a lost pale face.

I learnt when the tears
trickle down the stem
it's helping them,
they'll feel better afterwards.

The way our gardens grew,
so different.

Tears

A deep blue sea spills,
scarcely, they drop
from the frowns,
so unforgiving.

Oh, my clumsy soul,
always misplaces.
The dejected look I had
forged into a smile,
thanks dad.

The way our gardens grew,
so different.

Adolescence

/adə'lɛs(ə)ns/

Noun

Adolescence is a time in which I believe thinking and reasoning is a particularly significant part, you SHOULD start to make your own choices, stick up for yourself more and in general gain more freedoms.

I would say I am still going through *adolescence* at 20 years old. This is because I have previously struggled to make decisions that involve my own happiness being conflicted and therefore are usually made easier by simply accommodating other people first. I also struggle with situations that arise involving confrontation as I'm inclined to react in ways I would when I was a child. Being mindful of this and subsequently dealing with these things in a more mature and assured way makes me feel as if my inner child is being comforted. This is because I can see myself growing from that and backing myself more, as I should. Other people perhaps might take their responses for granted because they've had an upbringing where they wouldn't be required to think critically like this.

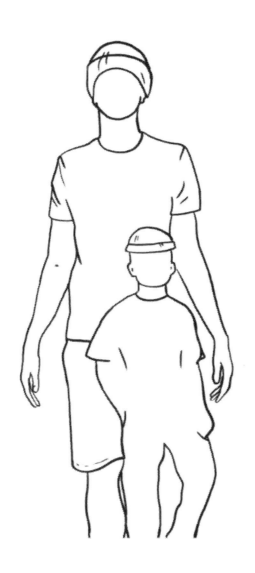

Adolescence

No preparation
for the mourning
as you still guide me,
unwanted.

Void of emotion,
I concede
when you tell me what to do -
the boy, still in there.

The way our gardens grew,
so different.

Adolescence

I let myself go
into the clouds of steam
I let off,
they surrender to judgement.

When you cross this line,
I won't stay hidden.
The almighty apprise,
a hefty price to pay.

The way our gardens grew,
so different.

Nana

/ˈnɑːnə/

Noun

One's Grandmother

It is fair to say that *Nanas* are often the best at making you feel comfortable and welcome. They would do anything for you. Whether you have one grandmother or two, their company is matchless. I was very lucky to meet my other grandmother just a year ago and it has been the most refreshing experience of my life. Having someone who doesn't judge me and has shown me the exact same love and care as she does her other grandchildren she has been in touch with considerably longer. To add, I think having a mature female figure in my life at a busy and stressful time has been beneficial. Having the sympathy and affection there is nice sometimes.

Nana

Your smile,
so incomparable
even when there's distance,
a consolatory ending.

The boxes of biscuits,
cups of tea
a prick at the malaise,
from the confidant.

The way our gardens grew,
so different.

Nana

Out she comes
from vines of ivy,
'dinners ready'
a feast unimaginable.

Her pride and joy,
the garden.
Weeds jealous of
the perfume from the
hyacinth overhang.

The way our gardens grew,
so different.

'Just forget about it'

To put it another way, 'try to erase something from your memory'.

This has been said to me a number of times, whether by relatives, friends or other people. It can come across as slightly cruel, even if that's not the intention behind saying it. It may just plainly be because some people don't have an understanding of ill mental health. It would be great in some instances to forget things or erase your roots but it's not as easy as that. They're there now, you can't change them. When it's said, you begin to question yourself and your perspective. Despite any of that, you should know that if it means something to you, it should remain. Don't let anyone tell you otherwise.

'Just forget about it'

Anchored in the soil,
everything absorbed,
some firmer than others,
but still in the ground.

When they're pulled out,
how the stem crumbles
under the eyes
of the unsettled sprout.

The way our gardens grew,
so different.

'Just forget about it'

We move on sometimes
to grow
in golden rays of sunlight-
you can forgive me for that.

I shall forgive you,
we can start over,
pale like our petals,
a blank page.

The way our gardens grew,
so different.

Today

/təˈdeɪ/

Noun

This present day

Today is a fresh start, a new chance, an opportunity to be positive and receive positivity back. If *today* is a bad day, sometimes it's best to accept it, and come back stronger tomorrow. Don't dwell on yesterday because it's gone. It was either an opportunity taken or wasted. If your *todays* feel miserable, take some time out for yourself, do something you enjoy, and don't let anyone take it away from you. Sometimes it's okay to be selfish, especially if it benefits your wellbeing.

You never know what will happen next. Life is unpredictable. Show love and care to your garden. Even if it wasn't looked after in the past, it can still grow into something quite remarkable. DO IT FOR YOU.

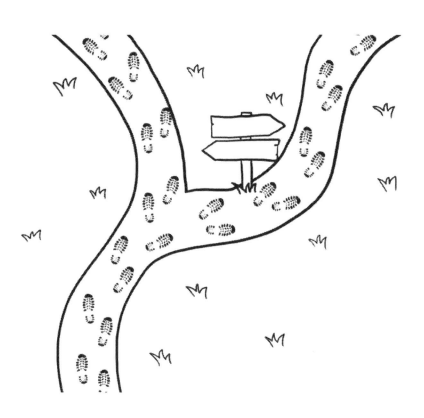

Today

This path is long,
pain fades
when I push him away,
I can feel myself,

Embrace adulthood,
I'm in control now.
If I have to, I'll look after him,
tell him everything is okay.
And we're on the same path now...

The way our gardens GROW,
so different.

Today

On this path
we work hard
for our goals are so different
we always keep faith

Unnerved by the future,
opportunities so bleak.
But we will find the key,
that fits the lock on the door.

The way our gardens GROW,
so different.

Thank you for reading and I hope this book provides you with the comfort and an insight into the idea that how you are planted isn't necessarily how you should grow, it can be extremely hard sometimes to drop things when you can always see a piece of them in you. I hope this reading can help you in some way, however it doesn't intend to provide treatment for you.

About the Author

Piers Eastwood is a 20 year old poet, writer and author from Manchester, he is an Undergraduate English Language with Creative Writing student at De Montfort University, Leicester. With three years experience in the writing world, Piers has shown expertise in Ekphrastic poetry and free verse. His main collection was 'The Silent Windmill' consisting of 6 free verse war poems. Piers' work broadly addresses stories of human emotions and behaviours.

Printed in Great Britain
by Amazon